PIANO • VOCAL • GUITAR

Avalon

A MAZE OF GRACE

ISBN 0-7935-9459-6

HAL•LEONARD®
CORPORATION
7777 W. BLUEMOUND RD. P.O. BOX 13819 MILWAUKEE, WI 53213

Visit Hal Leonard Online at
www.halleonard.com

Avalon
A MAZE OF GRACE

CONTENTS

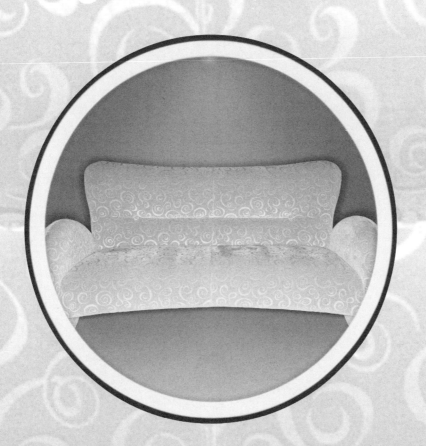

TESTIFY TO LOVE

Words and Music by PAUL FIELD, HENK POOL,
RALPH VAN MANEN and ROBERT RIEKERK

A WORLD AWAY

Words and Music by CHARLIE PEACOCK, NIKKI HASSMAN,
JODY McBRAYER, MICHAEL PASSONS and JANNA POTTER

I've been

A MAZE OF GRACE

Words and Music by GRANT CUNNINGHAM
and CHARLIE PEACOCK

KNOCKIN' ON HEAVEN'S DOOR

Words and Music by GRANT CUNNINGHAM
and MATT HUESMANN

ADONAI

Words and Music by LORRAINE FERRO,
DON KOCH and STEPHANIE LEWIS

SPEED OF LIGHT

Words and Music by MATT HUESMANN,
JODY McBRAYER, KYLE MATTHEWS and MICHAEL PASSONS

It's 3 A.M. ___ and you're toss - ing in ___ your bed. ___ Thoughts are turn -
Well, I've heard it said ___ that the peace of mind ___ that you ___ de - sire is ___ in the pow -

50

THE MOVE

Words and Music by MARGARET BECKER,
CHARLIE PEACOCK and RICK WILL

REASON ENOUGH

Words and Music by TY LACY,
JOHN MANDEVILLE and SHELLI MANDEVILLE

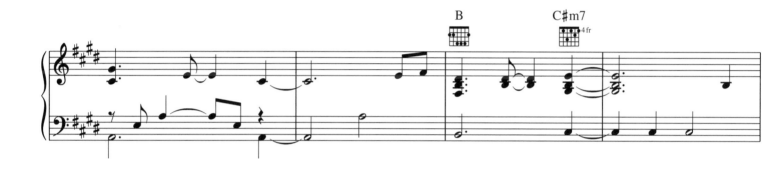

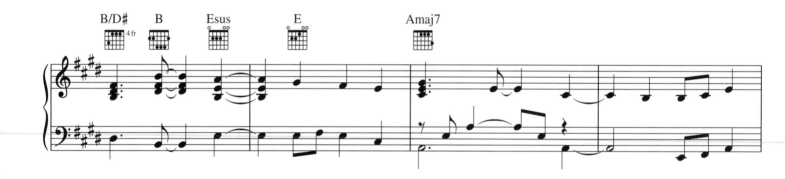

I don't know ___ what You saw

FORGIVE + FORGET

Words and Music by GRANT CUNNINGHAM
and MATT HUESMANN

(1.-3.) I won't __ for-get, Lord, __ that You will __ for-give me, __ or
(2.-4.) What I ___ re-gret, Lord, __ I will not __ re-gret, Lord. __ I

1-3

4

will that __ af-fect, Lord, __ the way? You for -
will not __ for-get, Lord, __ that You...

give.

I won't for-get that You for-give me.
Vocals 1st time only

DREAMS I DREAM FOR YOU

Words and Music by DOUGLAS McKELVEY
and CHARLIE PEACOCK

* Male voice written one octave lower than sung.